1,000,000 Books
are available to read at

Forgotten Books

www.ForgottenBooks.com

Read online
Download PDF
Purchase in print

ISBN 978-1-334-47082-0
PIBN 10740482

This book is a reproduction of an important historical work. Forgotten Books uses state-of-the-art technology to digitally reconstruct the work, preserving the original format whilst repairing imperfections present in the aged copy. In rare cases, an imperfection in the original, such as a blemish or missing page, may be replicated in our edition. We do, however, repair the vast majority of imperfections successfully; any imperfections that remain are intentionally left to preserve the state of such historical works.

Forgotten Books is a registered trademark of FB &c Ltd.
Copyright © 2018 FB &c Ltd.
FB &c Ltd, Dalton House, 60 Windsor Avenue, London, SW19 2RR.
Company number 08720141. Registered in England and Wales.

For support please visit www.forgottenbooks.com

1 MONTH OF FREE READING

at

www.ForgottenBooks.com

By purchasing this book you are eligible for one month membership to ForgottenBooks.com, giving you unlimited access to our entire collection of over 1,000,000 titles via our web site and mobile apps.

To claim your free month visit:

www.forgottenbooks.com/free740482

* Offer is valid for 45 days from date of purchase. Terms and conditions apply.

English
Français
Deutsche
Italiano
Español
Português

www.forgottenbooks.com

Mythology Photography **Fiction**
Fishing Christianity **Art** Cooking
Essays Buddhism Freemasonry
Medicine **Biology** Music **Ancient Egypt** Evolution Carpentry Physics
Dance Geology **Mathematics** Fitness
Shakespeare **Folklore** Yoga Marketing
Confidence Immortality Biographies
Poetry **Psychology** Witchcraft
Electronics Chemistry History **Law**
Accounting **Philosophy** Anthropology
Alchemy Drama Quantum Mechanics
Atheism Sexual Health **Ancient History**
Entrepreneurship Languages Sport
Paleontology Needlework Islam
Metaphysics Investment Archaeology
Parenting Statistics Criminology
Motivational

Issued July 29, 1912.

U. S. DEPARTMENT OF AGRICULTURE,
BUREAU OF STATISTICS—CIRCULAR 31.

VICTOR H. OLMSTED, Chief of Bureau.

ANNUAL AND AVERAGE PRODUCTION OF AND INTERNATIONAL TRADE IN IMPORTANT AGRICULTURAL PRODUCTS, BY COUNTRIES.

COMPILED BY

ROYAL T. McKENNA

From Yearbooks of the Department of Agriculture.

41668°—Cir. 31—12——1   WASHINGTON : GOVERNMENT PRINTING OFFICE : 1912

LETTER OF TRANSMITTAL.

U. S. DEPARTMENT OF AGRICULTURE,
BUREAU OF STATISTICS,
Washington, D. C., March 21, 1912.

SIR: I have the honor to transmit herewith manuscript prepared by Royal T. McKenna, of this bureau, which contains a compilation, first, of the annual and average production of important agricultural products in the leading producing countries, with the percentage which each contributes to the so-called "world" production; second, similar data respecting exports of certain agricultural products; and, third, data respecting imports of certain agricultural products.

The compilation is useful for ready reference. Much of the current information of crop production and movement is unintelligible to the average reader, because comparative figures are not given. Statistical data are of comparative value; for instance, a statement of the yield of wheat in Russia this year would have little value to most persons until they learned the average yield to which this year's yield may be compared, and, also, the relative importance of Russia as a wheat-producing country.

To supply such data for comparison this manuscript has been prepared, which I recommend to be published as Circular No. 31 of the Bureau of Statistics, entitled "Annual and Average Production of and International Trade in Important Agricultural Products, by Countries."

Very respectfully,

VICTOR H. OLMSTED,
Chief of Bureau.

Hon. JAMES WILSON,
Secretary of Agriculture.

CONTENTS.

	Page.
Corn	9
Wheat	10
Wheat flour	12
Oats	12
Barley	13
Rye	13
Potatoes	14
Cotton	14
Cottonseed oil	16
Tobacco	16
Flaxseed	18
Rice	19
Hops	21
Sugar	23
Tea	25
Coffee	25
Oil cake and oil-cake meal	27
Rosin	27
Turpentine	28
India rubber	28
Wood pulp	28
Average production of and international trade in important agricultural products	29
Rank of the United States in the production of and international trade in specified products	30

ANNUAL AND AVERAGE PRODUCTION OF AND INTERNATIONAL TRADE IN IMPORTANT AGRICULTURAL PRODUCTS, BY COUNTRIES.

Annual statistics of production and distribution, to have practical value, must be correlated with comparable statistics. A statement that a specified country has produced this year 100,000,000 bushels of wheat has in itself little meaning. The query naturally arises: Is this production unusually large, indicating a liberal supply, or does it indicate a short supply, likely to cause a tendency toward higher prices? The mere statement of the year's production does not give sufficient information to answer the queries.

Furthermore, is the country in question an important factor, either in the production or in the international trade in this product?

Crop news, especially that which appears in the daily or weekly press, frequently contains bare facts relative to the indicated production of a specified country, without comparative data. Traders, who are constantly engaged in the business, may be able to comprehend such information readily, but many readers, although interested in the subject, may not be similarly well informed nor have the necessary comparative data in hand. For the purpose of having in convenient form data of the average production of and trade in certain crops in important countries, the following tables have been prepared.

Late, and, in most cases, official data have been used in every instance.

The figures of production in the United States relate only to continental United States, except that those relating to coffee and sugar production include Porto Rico and Hawaii.

The expression "world's total production" of crops, used as in trade circles, includes only countries for which trustworthy data are available. Official data can be obtained from most Governments, but there are a few large countries for which the official data are incomplete; and some, such as China and Persia, for which official data of production are lacking.

In the figures of "world" crop production the crops of wheat and flaxseed harvested in the Southern Hemisphere from November to February of any year are coupled with those harvested in the Northern Hemisphere in the succeeding autumn.

Statistics of the exports and imports of products specified in this circular represent substantially the international trade of the world. It should not be expected that the totals of the world's exports and imports in the same year will agree. Among sources of disagreement are these: (1) Imports received in the year subsequent to year of export; (2) different periods of time covered in the year of the various countries; (3) lack of uniformity among different countries in the classification of goods; (4) different practices and varying degrees of failure in recording countries of origin and ultimate destination; (5) different practices of recording reexported goods; (6) different methods of treating free ports.

The exports given are of domestic produce, with a few exceptions, and the imports are imports for consumption as far as it is feasible and consistent so to express the facts. While there are some inevitable omissions, on the other hand there are some duplications because of reshipments that do not appear as such in official reports. For the United Kingdom import figures refer to imports for consumption, when available, otherwise total imports less exports of "foreign and colonial merchandise."

The exports and imports of the United States include Alaska, Porto Rico, and Hawaii.

A revision of the international trade tables is now being made in the Division of Production and Distribution of the Bureau of Statistics. This revision seems advisable on account of (1) a change in the official equivalent of the kilogram recently adopted by the bureau; (2) a failure in a few cases to use exactly the same classification from year to year for such composite groups as sugar, wool, and oil cake; (3) new returns received from important countries. The revised totals for world's exports and imports will therefore differ slightly in some cases from the totals published in the Yearbooks of the department and used in this circular. This revision is being made as rapidly as practicable.

CORN.

[Exports and imports include corn meal.]

Year.	Annual production (crop years).			Annual exports (including corn meal) (calendar years).			Annual imports (including corn meal) (calendar years).[a]
	"World."	United States.	Per cent of "world" crop grown in United States.	"World."	United States.	Per cent of "world" exports from United States.	"World."
	Bushels.	Bushels.	Per cent.	Bushels.	Bushels.	Per cent.	Bushels.
1911		2,531,488,000					
1910	4,026,967,000	2,886,260,000	71.7	230,691,819	44,072,209	19.1	221,921,839
1909	3,557,150,000	2,552,190,000	71.7	218,596,958	38,114,100	17.4	210,786,283
1908	3,608,822,000	2,668,651,000	73.9	188,192,445	39,013,273	20.7	187,346,478
1907	3,420,180,000	2,592,320,000	75.8	265,699,656	86,524,012	32.6	269,875,953
1906	3,928,947,000	2,927,416,000	74.5	267,700,656	105,258,629	39.3	268,578,783
1905	3,461,181,000	2,707,994,000	78.2	230,815,345	113,189,271	49.0	242,839,690
1904	3,109,252,000	2,467,481,000	79.4	204,946,752	47,896,231	23.4	217,500,714
1903	3,066,506,000	2,244,177,000	73.2	252,872,525	94,466,632	37.4	258,874,367
1902	3,187,311,000	2,523,648,000	79.2	177,160,970	19,749,404	11.1	210,483,315
1901	2,366,883,000	1,522,520,000	64.3	238,150,857	105,080,449	44.1	249,785,407
1900	2,792,561,000	2,105,103,000	75.4				
Average:							
1905–1909	3,595,256,000	2,689,714,000	74.8	234,201,012	76,419,857	32.6	235,885,037
1900–1904	2,904,503,000	2,172,586,000	74.8	218,282,776	[b]66,798,179	[b]30.6	[b]234,175,951
1895–1899	2,758,622,000	2,068,062,000	75.0				

[a] United States imports average less than 0.01 per cent of "world" imports.   [b] Four years.

AVERAGE ANNUAL PRODUCTION, 1905–1909 (CROP YEARS).

Country.	Bushels.	Per cent of "world" production.
United States	2,689,714,000	74.8
Austria-Hungary	189,547,000	5.3
Argentina	144,120,000	4.0
Mexico	131,322,000	3.7
Italy	94,806,000	2.6
Roumania	79,285,000	2.2
Russia (European)	51,061,000	1.4
Egypt	51,000,000	1.4
Spain	24,503,000	.7
Servia	23,095,000	.6
Other countries	116,803,000	3.3
"World" total	3,595,256,000	100.0

AVERAGE ANNUAL EXPORTS, 1905–1909 (CALENDAR YEARS).

Country.	Bushels.	Per cent of "world" exports.
Argentina	80,137,642	34.2
United States	76,419,857	32.6
Roumania	27,594,153	11.8
Russia	21,193,116	9.0
Belgium	7,106,983	3.0
Netherlands	6,554,204	2.8
Bulgaria	5,831,439	2.5
Servia	2,461,923	1.1
Austria-Hungary	127,152	.1
Uruguay	110,317	.1
Other countries	6,664,226	2.8
"World" total	234,201,012	100.0

10   PRODUCTION AND TRADE IN AGRICULTURAL PRODUCTS.

AVERAGE ANNUAL IMPORTS, 1905–1909 (CALENDAR YEARS).

Country.	Bushels.	Per cent of "world" imports.
United Kingdom	86,969,006	36.9
Germany	36,984,132	15.7
Netherlands	23,781,576	10.1
Belgium	21,811,813	9.2
France	12,665,125	5.4
Canada	11,035,392	4.7
Denmark	10,339,119	4.4
Austria-Hungary	7,374,045	3.1
Italy	5,766,448	2.4
Spain	3,767,077	1.6
Other countries	15,391,304	6.5
"World" total	235,885,037	100.0

WHEAT.

Year.	Wheat.			Wheat (including wheat flour reduced to its wheat equivalent).			Annual imports (calendar years).a
	Annual production (crop years).			Annual exports (calendar years).			
	"World."	United States.	Per cent of "world" crop grown in United States.	"World."	United States.	Per cent of "world" exports from United States.	"World."
	Bushels.	Bushels.		Bushels.	Bushels.		Bushels.
1911	3,516,862,000	621,338,000	17.7				
1910	3,572,084,000	635,121,000	17.8	711,514,048	61,923,296	8.7	666,262,913
1909	3,584,793,000	683,350,000	19.1	687,017,630	92,085,642	13.4	644,830,197
1908	3,181,548,000	664,602,000	20.9	573,109,085	151,338,121	26.4	555,523,822
1907	3,133,967,000	634,087,000	20.2	630,908,586	160,127,925	25.4	621,242,069
1906	3,434,354,000	735,261,000	21.4	626,307,018	127,309,434	20.3	618,977,529
1905	3,327,084,000	692,979,000	20.8	670,168,130	71,788,579	10.7	635,933,133
1904	3,163,542,000	552,400,000	17.5	605,329,724	64,957,058	10.7	574,180,892
1903	3,189,813,000	637,822,000	20.0	592,646,103	161,371,655	27.2	597,829,274
1902	3,090,116,000	670,063,000	21.7	537,732,995	202,905,598	37.6	543,708,452
1901	2,955,975,000	748,460,000	25.3	535,660,252	234,772,516	43.8	526,433,772
Average:							
1906–1910	3,381,349,000	670,484,000	19.8	645,771,273	118,556,884	18.4	621,367,306
1901–1905	3,145,306,000	660,345,000	21.0	588,307,441	147,159,081	25.0	575,617,105

a Annual imports of wheat, including wheat flour, into the United States, 1906–1910, average, 528,868 bushels.

AVERAGE ANNUAL PRODUCTION, 1906–1910 (CROP YEARS).

Country.	Bushels.	Per cent of "world" production.
United States	670,484,000	19.8
Russia (European)	557,757,000	16.5
France	326,709,000	9.7
British India	301,474,000	8.9
Austria-Hungary	222,394,000	6.6
Italy	169,874,000	5.0
Argentina	154,117,000	4.6
Germany	138,185,000	4.1
Canada	129,926,000	3.8
Spain	128,502,000	3.8
Other countries	581,927,000	17.2
"World" total	3,381,349,000	100.0

PRODUCTION AND TRADE IN AGRICULTURAL PRODUCTS. 11

AVERAGE ANNUAL EXPORTS, 1906-1910 (CALENDAR YEARS).
[Wheat, including flour reduced to its wheat equivalent.]

Country.	Bushels.	Per cent of "world" exports.
Russia	141,497,008	21.9
United States	118,556,884	18.4
Argentina	101,353,057	15.7
Canada	54,566,596	8.4
Roumania	40,723,958	6.3
Netherlands	43,584,178	6.7
Australia	37,262,006	5.8
British India	30,551,110	4.7
Belgium	23,207,280	3.6
Germany	14,317,564	2.2
Other countries	40,151,632	6.3
"World" total	645,771,273	100.0

AVERAGE ANNUAL IMPORTS, 1906-1910 (CALENDAR YEARS).
[Wheat, including flour reduced to its wheat equivalent.]

Country.	Bushels.	Per cent of "world" imports.
United Kingdom	211,374,064	34.0
Germany	84,129,369	13.5
Belgium	69,883,995	11.2
Netherlands	63,417,912	10.2
Italy	41,669,212	6.7
Brazil	17,011,146	2.7
Switzerland	14,981,560	2.4
France	11,659,683	1.9
Egypt	8,052,323	1.3
Sweden	7,435,461	1.2
Other countries	91,752,581	14.9
"World" total	621,367,306	100.0

WHEAT AND WHEAT FLOUR.

Calendar year.	Wheat.				Wheat flour.			
	Annual exports.			Annual imports.	Annual exports.			Annual imports.
	"World."	United States.	Per cent of "world" exports from United States.	"World" imports.	"World."	United States.	Per cent of "world" exports from United States.	"World."
	Bushels.	Bushels.		Bushels.	Barrels.	Barrels.		Barrels.
1910	604,610,900	24,257,392	4.0	573,681,187	23,756,255	8,370,201	35.2	20,573,717
1909	581,869,176	48,489,674	8.3	547,938,348	23,366,323	9,687,993	41.5	21,531,522
1908	464,336,899	92,779,509	20.0	446,776,880	24,171,597	13,013,025	53.8	24,165,987
1907	510,776,805	91,383,648	17.9	506,330,813	26,695,951	15,276,506	57.2	25,535,835
1906	513,163,514	62,850,984	12.2	510,476,503	25,143,001	14,324,100	57.0	24,111,339
1905	567,581,905	20,738,635	3.7	540,124,116	22,796,939	11,344,432	49.8	21,290,893
1904	510,629,798	13,015,277	2.5	481,241,816	21,044,428	11,542,618	54.8	20,653,128
1903	470,794,270	73,372,755	15.6	479,972,492	27,078,185	19,555,311	72.2	26,190,396
1902	435,180,608	129,466,280	29.8	441,460,297	24,798,338	18,328,767	73.9	22,721,812
1901	448,404,972	179,201,418	40.0	414,111,705	26,393,259	19,352,330	73.3	24,960,460
Average:								
1906-1910	534,951,459	63,952,241	12.0	517,040,746	24,626,625	12,134,365	49.3	23,183,680
1901-1905	486,518,311	83,158,873	17.1	471,382,085	24,422,230	16,024,692	65.6	23,163,338

a Annual imports of wheat into the United States, 1906-1910, average 187,083 bushels.
b Annual imports of wheat flour into the United States, 1906-1910, average 88,000 barrels.

WHEAT.

Average annual exports, 1906–1910 (calendar years).			Average annual imports, 1906–1910 (calendar years).		
Country.	Bushels.	Per cent of "world" exports.	Country.	Bushels.	Per cent of "world" imports.
Russia	137,288,875	25.7	United Kingdom	180,013,118	34.8
Argentina	95,259,969	17.8	Germany	83,263,166	16.1
United States	63,952,241	12.0	Belgium	69,714,213	13.5
Canada	44,799,010	8.4	Netherlands	53,824,415	10.4
Netherlands	42,705,672	8.0	Italy	41,599,589	8.0
Roumania	39,013,949	7.3	Switzerland	14,981,560	2.9
Australia	30,677,049	5.7	France	11,148,944	2.2
British India	28,697,278	5.4	Brazil	9,237,675	1.8
Belgium	20,765,090	3.9	Austria-Hungary	7,803,207	1.5
Bulgaria	8,224,244	1.5	Spain	7,193,704	1.4
Germany	7,705,491	1.4	Greece	7,133,803	1.4
Other countries	15,862,591	2.9	Other countries	31,127,352	6.0
"World" total	534,951,459	100.0	"World" total	517,040,746	100.0

WHEAT FLOUR.

Average annual exports, 1906–1910 (calendar years).			Average annual imports, 1906–1910 (calendar years).		
Country.	Barrels.	Per cent of "world" exports.	Country.	Barrels.	Per cent of "world" imports.
United States	12,134,365	49.3	United Kingdom	6,969,099	30.1
Canada	2,170,575	8.8	Netherlands	2,131,888	9.2
Germany	1,469,350	6.0	Brazil	1,727,438	7.5
Australia	1,463,323	5.9	Egypt	1,694,130	7.3
Argentina	1,354,020	5.5	China	1,264,302	5.5
Russia	935,141	3.8	Finland	966,020	4.2
United Kingdom	756,575	3.1	Cuba	807,685	3.5
Belgium	542,709	2.2	Norway	553,263	2.4
Italy	499,778	2.0	Japan	529,870	2.3
British India	411,962	1.7	Denmark	443,981	1.9
Other countries	2,888,827	11.7	Other countries	6,096,004	26.1
"World" total	24,626,625	100.0	"World" total	23,183,680	100.0

OATS.

	Annual production.			Average annual production, 1906–1910.		
Crop year.	"World."	United States.	Per cent of "world" crop grown in United States.	Country.	Bushels.	Per cent of "world" production.
	Bushels.	Bushels.				
1911	3,820,226,000	922,298,000	24.1	United States	943,995,000	24.4
1910	4,214,727,000	1,186,341,000	28.1	Russia (European)	864,765,000	22.3
1909	4,379,287,000	1,007,129,000	23.0	Germany	582,867,000	15.1
1908	3,603,798,000	807,156,000	22.4	Canada	294,920,000	7.6
1907	3,603,896,000	754,443,000	20.9	France	293,726,000	7.6
1906	3,544,961,000	964,905,000	27.2	Austria-Hungary	246,253,000	6.4
1905	3,510,167,000	953,216,000	27.2	United Kingdom	185,445,000	4.8
1904	3,611,302,000	894,596,000	24.8	Russia (Asiatic)	85,847,000	2.2
1903	3,378,034,000	784,094,000	23.2	Sweden	69,290,000	1.8
1902	3,626,303,000	987,843,000	27.2	Denmark	40,892,000	1.1
1901	2,862,615,000	736,809,000	25.7	Belgium	42,491,000	1.1
				Other countries	218,843,000	5.6
Average:				"World" total	3,869,334,000	100.0
1906–1910	3,869,334,000	943,995,000	24.4			
1901–1905	3,397,684,000	871,312,000	25.6			

PRODUCTION AND TRADE IN AGRICULTURAL PRODUCTS. 13

BARLEY.

Crop year.	Annual production.			Average annual production, 1906-1910.		
	"World."	United States.	Per cent of "world" crop grown in United States.	Country.	Bushels.	Per cent of "world" production.
	Bushels.	Bushels.				
1911	1,379,598,000	160,240,000	11.6	European Russia	385,880,	28.8
1910	1,383,192,000	173,832,000	12.6	United States	169,284,	12.6
1909	1,477,502,000	173,321,000	11.7	Germany	147,594,	11.0
1908	1,264,803,000	166,756,000	13.2	Austria-Hungary	142,761,	10.7
1907	1,271,237,000	153,597,000	12.1	Japanese Empire	86,195,	6.5
1906	1,296,579,000	178,916,000	13.8	Spain	74,269,	5.5
1905	1,180,053,000	136,651,000	11.6	United Kingdom	67,707,	5.1
1904	1,175,784,000	139,749,000	11.9	Canada	48,202,	3.6
1903	1,235,786,000	131,861,000	10.7	Algeria	43,874,	3.3
1902	1,229,132,000	134,954,000	11.0	France	41,975,000	3.1
1901	1,072,195,000	109,933,000	10.3	Other countries	130,922,000	9.8
Average:				"World"		
1906-1910	1,338,663,000	169,284,000	12.6	total	1,338,663,000	100.0
1901-1905	1,178,590,000	130,630,000	11.1			

RYE.

Crop year.	Annual production.			Average annual production, 1906-1910.		
	"World."	United States.	Per cent of "world" crop grown in United States.	Country.	Bushels.	Per cent of "world" production.
	Bushels.	Bushels.				
1911	1,579,768,000	33,119,000	2.1	Russia (European).	778,483,000	48.8
1910	1,668,937,000	34,897,000	2.1	Germany	409,272,000	25.7
1909	1,742,466,000	29,520,000	1.7	Austria-Hungary	153,304,000	9.6
1908	1,589,299,000	31,851,000	2.0	France	51,405,000	3.2
1907	1,538,778,000	31,566,000	2.1	United States	32,242,000	2.0
1906	1,433,395,000	33,375,000	2.3	Spain	29,371,000	1.8
1905	1,495,751,000	28,486,000	1.9	Russia (Asiatic)	25,810,000	1.6
1904	1,742,112,000	27,242,000	1.6	Sweden	24,770,000	1.6
1903	1,659,961,000	29,363,000	1.8	Belgium	22,298,000	1.4
1902	1,647,845,000	33,631,000	2.0	Denmark	18,476,000	1.2
1901	1,416,022,000	30,345,000	2.1	Netherlands	15,413,000	1.0
				Other countries	33,731,000	2.1
Average:				"World"		
1906-1910	1,594,575,000	32,242,000	2.0	total	1,594,575,000	100.0
1901-1905	1,592,338,000	29,813,000	1.9			

POTATOES.

Crop year.	Annual production.			Average annual production, 1905-1909.		
	"World."	United States.	Per cent of "world" crop grown in United States.	Country.	Bushels.	Per cent of "world" production.
	Bushels.	Bushels.				
1911		292,737,000		Germany	1,689,085,000	32.5
1910	5,196,715,000	349,032,000	6.7	Russia (European)	1,048,067,000	20.2
1909	5,536,522,000	389,195,000	7.0			
1908	5,273,584,000	278,985,000	5.3	Austria-Hungary	709,165,000	13.7
1907	5,121,222,000	298,262,000	5.8	France	529,249,000	10.2
1906	4,789,112,000	308,038,000	6.4	United States	307,044,000	5.9
1905	5,254,598,000	260,741,000	5.0	United Kingdom	242,630,000	4.7
1904	4,298,049,000	332,830,000	7.7	Netherlands	94,184,000	1.8
1903	4,409,793,000	247,128,000	5.6	Spain	85,403,000	1.6
1902	4,674,000,000	284,633,000	6.1	Belgium	79,939,000	1.5
1901	4,669,958,000	187,598,000	4.0	Canada	72,035,000	1.4
1900	4,382,031,000	210,927,000	4.8	Other countries	338,207,000	6.5
Average:				"World" total	5,195,008,000	100.0
1905-1909	5,195,008,000	307,044,000	5.9			
1900-1904	4,486,766,000	252,623,000	5.6			

COTTON.

[Bales of 500 pounds, gross weight, or 478 pounds of lint, net.]

Crop year.	Annual production.			Annual exports (calendar years).			Annual imports (calendar years).		
	World.	United States.a	Per cent of "world" crop grown in United States.	World.	United States.	Per cent of "world" exports from United States.	World.	United States.	Per cent of "world" imports into United States.
	Bales.	Bales.	Per cent.	Bales.	Bales.	Per cent.	Bales.	Bales.	Per cent.
1910	19,992,780	11,608,616	58.1	12,424,064	7,289,806	58.7	12,262,384	178,409	1.5
1909	18,051,685	10,004,949	55.4	12,683,027	8,149,477	64.3	13,158,212	193,940	1.5
1908	21,320,793	13,241,799	62.1	12,995,848	9,152,070	70.4	12,655,018	154,662	1.2
1907	18,820,925	11,107,179	59.0	13,692,706	8,769,988	64.0	13,617,895	236,293	1.7
1906	22,108,645	13,273,809	60.0	11,807,624	7,700,458	65.2	11,532,746	137,415	1.2
1905	18,342,075	10,575,017	57.7	12,297,518	8,310,524	67.6	12,075,230	142,982	1.2
1904	21,005,175	13,438,012	64.0	10,701,729	6,801,689	63.6	10,926,922	102,529	.9
1903	17,278,881	9,851,129	57.0	10,887,466	7,296,145	67.0	10,947,408	132,209	1.2
1902	17,331,503	10,630,945	61.3	10,810,171	7,144,231	66.1	10,632,583	178,592	1.7
1901	15,926,048	9,509,745	59.7	10,755,334	7,433,846	69.1	10,345,161	142,817	1.4
1900	15,893,591	10,123,027	63.7	10,030,020	7,108,578	70.9	9,695,969	126,607	1.3
Average:									
1905-1909	19,728,824	11,640,551	59.0	12,695,345	8,416,503	66.3	12,607,820	173,058	1.4
1900-1904	17,487,040	10,710,572	61.3	10,636,944	7,156,898	67.3	10,509,609	136,551	1.3

a Excluding linters.

PRODUCTION AND TRADE IN AGRICULTURAL PRODUCTS. 15

AVERAGE ANNUAL PRODUCTION, 1905-1909 (CROP YEARS).

Country.	Bales of 500 pounds, gross weight, or 478 pounds of lint, net.	Per cent of "world" production.
United States [a]	11,640,551	59.0
British India [b]	4,058,600	20.6
Egypt [c]	1,308,585	6.6
China	1,200,000	6.1
Russia (Asiatic) [d]	572,850	2.9
Brazil	298,200	1.5
Mexico	159,427	.8
Peru	112,255	.6
Persia [e]	95,014	.5
Turkey (Asiatic) [f]	79,600	.4
Other countries	203,742	1.0
"World" total	19,728,824	100.0

[a] An annual average production of 294,090 bales of linters for five-year period 1905-1909 not included.
[b] Net exports and consumption.
[c] Note that production is less than exports; apparently production is underestimated.
[d] Including Khiva and Bokhara.
[e] Exports.
[f] Anatolia and Adana only.

AVERAGE ANNUAL EXPORTS, 1905-1909 (CALENDAR YEARS).

Country.	Bales of 500 pounds, gross weight, or 478 pounds of lint, net.	Per cent of "world" exports.
United States	8,416,503	66.3
British India	1,736,172	13.7
Egypt	1,383,914	10.9
Germany	222,678	1.8
China	213,463	1.7
France	202,438	1.6
Netherlands	111,788	.9
Persia	95,014	.7
Brazil	89,770	.7
Peru	87,332	.7
Other countries	136,273	1.0
"World" total	12,695,345	100.0

AVERAGE ANNUAL IMPORTS, 1905-1909 (CALENDAR YEARS).

Country.	Bales of 500 pounds, gross weight, or 478 pounds of lint, net.	Per cent of "world" imports.
United Kingdom	3,945,076	31.3
Germany	2,100,434	16.7
France	1,250,302	9.9
Japan	1,025,778	8.1
Italy	888,893	7.1
Russia	863,555	6.9
Austria-Hungary	825,304	6.5
Spain	387,845	3.1
Belgium	258,280	2.0
Netherlands	229,033	1.8
Other countries	833,320	6.6
"World" total	12,607,820	100.0

COTTONSEED OIL.

Average annual exports, 1905–1909 (calendar years).			Average annual imports, 1905–1909 (calendar years)		
Country.	Gallons.	Per cent of "world" exports.	Country.	Gallons.	Per cent of "world" imports.
United States	45,445,357	82.5	Germany	14,158,311	25.7
United Kingdom	7,296,635	13.2	France	9,741,369	17.7
Belgium	1,237,630	2.3	Netherlands	5,310,218	9.6
France	622,855	1.1	Mexico	4,302,754	7.8
Egypt	290,801	.5	United Kingdom	4,134,803	7.5
Netherlands	132,707	.2	Italy	3,443,423	6.2
Other countries	30,565	.2	Belgium	2,565,108	4.7
			Austria-Hungary	2,325,089	4.2
			Canada	1,517,458	2.8
			Algeria	1,138,976	2.1
			Other countries	6,521,771	11.7
"World" total	55,056,550	100.0	"World" total	55,159,280	100.0

TOBACCO.a

AVERAGE ANNUAL PRODUCTION, 1905–1909 (CROP YEARS).

Country.	Pounds.	Per cent. of "world" production.
United States (including Porto Rico)	766,883,000	31.6
United States	757,483,000	31.3
British India	450,000,000	18.6
Russia (including Asiatic)	197,446,000	8.2
Austria-Hungary	169,524,000	7.0
Dutch East Indies a	148,972,000	6.1
Turkey (including Asiatic)	100,000,000	4.1
Japanese Empire	94,409,000	3.9
Germany	68,120,000	2.8
Brazil b	52,063,000	2.2
Cuba	51,797,000	2.1
Other countries	324,355,000	13.4
"World" total	2,423,569,000	100.0

ANNUAL PRODUCTION.

Crop year.	"World."	United States.	Per cent of "world" crop grown in United States.
	Pounds.	Pounds.	
1911		905,109,000	
1910	2,756,077,000	1,103,415,000	40.0
1909	2,693,894,000	1,055,765,000	39.2
1908	2,403,907,000	718,061,000	29.9
1907	2,418,177,000	698,126,000	28.9
1906	2,322,158,000	682,429,000	29.4
1905	2,279,728,000	633,034,000	27.8
1904	2,146,641,000	660,461,000	30.8
1903	2,401,268,000	815,972,000	34.0
1902	2,376,054,000	821,824,000	34.6
1901	2,270,213,000	818,953,000	36.1
1900	2,201,193,000	814,345,000	37.0
Average:			
1905–1909	2,423,569,000	757,483,000	31.3
1900–1904	2,279,074,000	786,311,000	34.5

a Export and import figures are for calendar years.

PRODUCTION AND TRADE IN AGRICULTURAL PRODUCTS. 17

ANNUAL EXPORTS (UNMANUFACTURED).

Calendar year.	"World."	United States.	Per cent of "world" exports from United States.
	Pounds.	Pounds.	
1910	836,142,651	328,562,036	39.3
1909	813,464,526	351,564,177	43.2
1908	764,299,982	305,455,871	40.0
1907	773,813,339	317,399,986	41.0
1906	777,948,332	336,730,455	43.3
1905	659,113,356	292,925,181	44.4
1904	705,736,277	349,331,687	49.5
1903	679,808,097	316,325,914	46.5
1902	752,021,052	364,069,340	48.4
1901	660,205,674	308,743,593	46.8
1900	615,626,599	305,033,235	49.5
Average:			
1905-1909	757,727,907	320,815,134	42.3
1900-1904	682,079,540	328,700,754	48.1

ANNUAL IMPORTS (UNMANUFACTURED).

Calendar year.	"World."	United States.	Per cent of "world" imports into United States.
	Pounds.	Pounds.	
1910	749,439,082	42,343,323	5.7
1909	739,571,200	44,221,940	6.0
1908	752,405,520	37,665,211	5.0
1907	728,212,062	34,088,288	4.7
1906	686,249,816	41,726,224	6.1
1905	723,428,467	33,887,947	4.7
1904	672,656,403	30,603,290	4.5
1903	648,524,246	32,997,923	5.1
1902	614,142,678	32,192,212	5.2
1901	626,052,079	28,017,550	4.5
1900	604,110,456	23,192,105	3.8
Average:			
1905-1909	725,973,413	38,317,922	5.3
1900-1904	633,097,172	29,400,616	4.6

AVERAGE ANNUAL EXPORTS (UNMANUFACTURED), 1905-1909 (CALENDAR YEARS).

Country.	Pounds.	Per cent of "world" exports.
United States	320,815,134	42.3
Dutch East Indies	146,525,006	19.3
Brazil	52,063,207	6.9
Turkey c	39,267,984	5.2
Cuba	34,018,364	4.5
Philippine Islands	23,202,516	3.1
British India	23,181,313	3.1
Austria-Hungary	20,384,157	2.7
Santo Domingo	18,658,000	2.5
Russia	17,204,449	2.3
Other countries	62,407,777	8.1
"World" total	757,727,907	100.0

PRODUCTION AND TRADE IN AGRICULTURAL PRODUCTS.

AVERAGE ANNUAL IMPORTS (UNMANUFACTURED), 1905-1909 (CALENDAR YEARS).

Country.	Pounds.	Per cent of "world" imports.
Germany	161,928,393	22.3
United Kingdom	85,425,596	11.8
France	58,484,234	8.1
Netherlands	47,864,305	6.6
Austria-Hungary	46,557,022	6.4
Italy	42,504,043	5.9
Spain	40,585,002	5.6
United States	38,317,922	5.3
Belgium	21,113,582	2.9
Egypt	18,290,606	2.5
Other countries	164,902,708	22.6
"World" total	725,973,413	100.0

a Exports 100,200,000 pounds for Java, and production of 48,772,000 pounds for Sumatra.
b Exports.
c Estimate based on data for year beginning Mar. 14, 1900.

FLAXSEED.

Crop year.	Annual production.			Average annual production, 1905-1909.		
	"World."	United States.	Per cent of "world" crop grown in United States.	Country.	Bushels.	Per cent of "world" production.
	Bushels.	*Bushels.*				
1911		19,370,000		Argentina	33,912,000	34.3
1910		12,718,000		United States	25,045,000	25.4
1909	100,943,000	19,513,000	19.3	Russia (European)	20,269,000	20.5
1908	100,850,000	25,805,000	25.6	British India	12,622,000	12.8
1907	102,960,000	25,851,000	25.1	Russia (Asiatic)	1,575,000	1.6
1906	88,165,000	25,576,000	29.0	Canada	1,445,000	1.5
1905	100,458,000	28,478,000	28.3	Austria-Hungary	1,408,000	1.4
1904	107,743,000	23,401,000	21.7	Uruguay	617,000	.6
1903	110,455,000	27,301,000	24.7	France	598,000	.6
1902	83,891,000	29,285,000	34.9	Netherlands	351,000	.4
1901	72,314,000	a 25,000,000	34.6	Belgium	295,000	.3
1900	62,432,000	a 18,000,000	28.8	Other countries	610,000	.6
Average:						
1905-1909	98,675,000	25,045,000	25.4	"World" total	98,675,000	100.0
1900-1904	87,367,000	24,597,000	28.2			

a Commercial estimate.

RICE a (MOSTLY CLEANED RICE).

Crop year.	Annual production.		
	World.	United States.a	Per cent of "world" crop grown in United States.
	Pounds.	*Pounds.*	
1911		637,056,000	
1910		680,833,000	
1909	135,186,068,000	676,889,000	0.5
1908	108,144,842,000	608,056,000	.6
1907	106,423,412,000	520,000,000	.5
1906	111,760,923,000	496,000,000	.4
1905	108,963,551,000	359,000,000	.3
1904	115,735,800,000	586,000,000	.5
1903	110,865,000,000	560,750,000	.5
1902	106,626,400,000	319,393,000	.3
1901	99,445,600,000	388,035,000	.4
1900	91,584,400,000	253,139,000	.3
Average:			
1905–1909	114,095,759,000	531,989,000	.5
1900–1904	104,851,440,000	421,463,000	.4

Calendar year.	Annual imports.			Annual "world" exports.b
	World.	United States.	Per cent of "world" exports from United States.	
	Pounds.	*Pounds.*		*Pounds.*
1910	11,880,376,821	224,826,350	1.9	13,170,720,622
1909	9,585,585,894	225,710,483	2.4	11,754,169,414
1908	10,272,989,071	217,345,610	2.1	11,448,571,827
1907	10,203,198,427	203,560,814	2.0	11,998,176,331
1906	9,600,989,962	209,152,583	2.2	10,483,776,764
1905	9,628,189,018	109,544,299	1.1	10,801,128,816
1904	10,301,400,308	136,587,147	1.3	11,852,915,120
1903	9,252,387,474	177,804,747	1.9	10,295,494,939
1902	10,130,678,027	165,407,322	1.6	12,011,983,506
1901	8,770,546,516	138,685,742	1.6	9,668,609,537
1900	7,190,368,880	105,119,077	1.5	8,375,629,013
Average:				
1905–1909	9,858,190,474	193,062,758	2.0	11,297,164,630
1900–1904	9,129,076,241	144,720,807	1.6	10,440,926,423

a Includes only Continental United States.
b Exports of rice from the United States to foreign countries for 1906-1910 average less than 4,000,000 pounds per annum; but the average annual shipments to Porto Rico, 1906-1910, average about 97,000,000 pounds.

20   PRODUCTION AND TRADE IN AGRICULTURAL PRODUCTS.

AVERAGE ANNUAL PRODUCTION,[a] 1905–1909 (CROP YEARS).

Country.	Pounds.	Per cent of "world" production.
British India [b]	69,720,400,000	61.1
Japanese Empire	17,644,119,000	15.5
Java	6,899,600,000	6.0
Siam	6,824,000,000	6.0
French Indo-China	5,000,000,000	4.4
Korea [c]	3,200,000,000	2.8
Madagascar	953,000,000	.8
Philippine Islands	716,000,000	.6
Italy	703,400,000	.6
United States (including Hawaii)	565,389,000	.5
United States	531,989,000	.5
Other countries	1,869,851,000	1.7
"World" total	114,095,759,000	100.0

AVERAGE ANNUAL EXPORTS, 1905–1909 (CALENDAR YEARS).

Country.	Pounds.	Per cent of "world" exports.
British India	4,249,459,576	37.6
French Indo-China	2,177,224,657	19.3
Siam	1,937,210,237	17.1
Singapore	758,025,271	6.7
Netherlands	330,838,501	2.9
Germany	308,945,219	2.7
Penang	305,229,571	2.7
Formosa	187,482,214	1.7
Dutch East Indies	113,028,881	1.0
France	82,711,935	.7
Other countries	847,008,568	7.6
"World" total	11,297,164,630	100.0

AVERAGE ANNUAL IMPORTS, 1905–1909 (CALENDAR YEARS).

Country.	Pounds.	Per cent of "world" imports.
Singapore	883,134,915	9.0
Japan	870,237,653	8.8
China	805,703,414	8.2
Germany	767,265,942	7.8
Dutch East Indies	709,550,294	7.2
Ceylon	686,380,839	7.0
United Kingdom	656,562,243	6.7
Netherlands	606,133,366	6.1
France	421,760,014	4.3
Philippine Islands	348,706,327	3.5
Other countries	3,102,755,467	31.4
"World" total	9,858,190,474	100.0

[a] The United States crop is computed from the official returns, which are for rough rice, allowing 45 pounds rough to 1 bushel, and 162 pounds rough to 100 pounds clean. China, which is omitted, has a roughly estimated crop of 50,000,000,000 to 60,000,000,000 pounds. Other countries omitted are Afghanistan, Algeria, Colombia, Federated Malay States, Persia, Trinidad and Tobago, Turkey (Asiatic and European), Venezuela, and a few other countries of small production.

[b] Data for British India refer to years beginning April 1 of the years mentioned in the heading. Production given here is estimated unofficially for the entire country on the basis of official returns for about 0.7 per cent of the area harvested.

[c] Estimated from official returns of exports of this country, and from per capita consumption of rice in Japan, 1894–1903, including food, seed, and waste, but not including rice used for sake (270 pounds per annum).

HOPS.
ANNUAL PRODUCTION.

Crop year.	"World." a	United States.	Per cent of "world" crop grown in United States.
	Pounds.	Pounds.	Per cent.
1911	147,315,000	40,000,000	27.2
1910	182,517,000	44,000,000	24.1
1909	116,389,000	40,000,000	34.4
1908	225,320,000	39,000,000	17.3
1907	212,413,000	54,000,000	25.4
1906	180,998,000	60,286,000	33.3
1905	277,260,000	55,536,000	20.0
1904	178,802,000	49,125,000	27.5
1903	174,457,000	44,295,000	25.4
1902	170,063,000	39,000,000	22.9
1901	201,902,000	38,800,000	19.2
Average:			
1906–1910	183,527,000	47,457,000	25.9
1901–1905	200,497,000	45,351,000	22.6

ANNUAL EXPORTS.

Calendar year.	"World."	United States.	Per cent of "world" exports from United States.
	Pounds.	Pounds.	Per cent.
1910	56,838,892	12,748,617	22.4
1909	55,261,865	8,955,533	16.2
1908	69,159,608	21,423,869	31.0
1907	62,969,084	16,090,959	25.6
1906	65,795,524	17,701,436	26.9
1905	55,185,057	5,713,682	10.4
1904	68,181,507	17,777,608	26.1
1903	47,003,388	9,199,448	19.6
1902	53,208,060	9,156,244	17.2
1901	55,032,255	9,915,434	18.0
Average:			
1906–1910	62,004,995	15,384,083	24.8
1901–1905	55,722,053	10,352,483	18.6

ANNUAL IMPORTS.

Calendar year.	"World."	United States.	Per cent of "world" imports into United States.
	Pounds.	Pounds.	Per cent.
1910	56,724,253	5,823,520	10.3
1909	56,336,718	6,807,689	12.1
1908	70,296,729	7,369,684	10.5
1907	62,121,955	7,163,356	11.5
1906	65,377,247	7,849,548	12.0
1905	52,357,226	5,968,533	11.4
1904	70,280,440	4,736,488	6.7
1903	48,118,352	3,885,974	8.1
1902	54,878,173	4,778,144	8.7
1901	53,588,435	2,669,045	5.0
Average:			
1906–1910	62,171,380	7,002,759	11.3
1901–1905	55,844,525	4,407,637	7.9

PRODUCTION AND TRADE IN AGRICULTURAL PRODUCTS.

AVERAGE ANNUAL PRODUCTION, 1906-1910 (CROP YEARS).

Country.	Pounds.	Per cent of "world" production.
United States a	47,457,000	25.9
Germany	43,213,000	23.5
United Kingdom	36,013,000	19.6
Austria-Hungary	30,130,000	16.4
Russia (European)	9,584,000	5.2
France	7,770,000	4.2
Belgium	6,405,000	3.5
Tasmania	1,284,000	.7
New Zealand b	927,000	.5
Victoria	181,000	.1
Other countries	563,000	.4
"World" total	183,527,000	100.0

a Production in the States of New York, California, Oregon, and Washington only, based on estimates of the "California Fruit Grower" and "American Agriculturist."
b Estimate based on official figures of area, multiplied by yield as given in census, 1895, 1,088 pounds. Data for 1909 used for 1910.

AVERAGE ANNUAL EXPORTS, 1906-1910 (CALENDAR YEARS).

Country.	Pounds.	Per cent of "world" exports.
Germany	23,034,652	37.1
Austria-Hungary	16,410,428	26.5
United States	15,384,083	24.8
Belgium	2,396,742	3.9
Netherlands	1,499,590	2.4
United Kingdom	1,255,834	2.0
Russia	1,249,272	2.0
New Zealand	329,504	.5
France	253,266	.4
Other countries	191,624	.4
"World" total	62,004,995	100.0

AVERAGE ANNUAL IMPORTS, 1906-1910 (CALENDAR YEARS).

Country.	Pounds.	Per cent of "world" imports.
United Kingdom	22,365,078	36.0
United States	7,002,759	11.3
Germany	6,538,791	10.5
Belgium	5,849,446	9.4
France	4,894,195	7.9
Netherlands	3,172,551	5.1
Russia	1,311,039	2.1
Denmark	1,215,249	2.0
Switzerland	1,191,462	1.9
Sweden	1,160,299	1.9
Other countries	7,470,511	11.9
"World" total	62,171,380	100.0

PRODUCTION AND TRADE IN AGRICULTURAL PRODUCTS. 23

SUGAR.

[Exports given are domestic exports; imports are imports for consumption.]

Crop year.	Annual production.				
	"World." a	United States (continental).	Per cent of "world" crop grown in United States (continental).	United States (including Hawaii and Porto Rico).	Per cent of "world" crop grown in United States.
	Long tons.	*Long tons.*		*Long tons.*	
1910–11	16,418,500	767,000	4.7	1,564,900	9.5
1909–10	14,524,450	746,250	5.1	1,488,750	10.2
1908–9	14,262,000	750,000	5.3	1,452,400	10.2
1907–8	13,665,900	766,000	5.6	1,417,000	10.4
1906–7	14,241,500	675,000	4.7	1,252,700	8.8
1905–6	13,964,988	628,145	4.5	1,224,370	8.8
1904–5	11,774,114	586,704	5.0	1,112,280	9.4
1903–4	12,271,659	463,102	3.8	921,205	7.5
1902–3	11,818,460	524,008	4.4	1,000,070	8.5
1901–2	13,000,822	484,802	3.7	887,311	6.8
Average:					
1906–7 to 1910–11	14,622,470	740,850	5.1	1,435,190	9.8
1901–2 to 1905–6	12,566,009	537,352	4.3	1,029,047	8.2

Calendar year.	Annual imports.			
	"World."	United States.	Per cent of "world" imports into United States.	Annual "world" exports. b
	Long tons.	*Long tons.*		*Long tons.*
1910	6,003,456	1,872,802	31.2	6,487,004
1909	5,926,598	1,703,972	28.8	6,337,738
1908	5,609,361	1,660,134	29.6	5,811,386
1907	5,700,743	1,728,670	30.3	6,085,277
1906	5,729,227	1,729,315	30.2	6,135,548
1905	5,004,526	1,668,454	33.3	5,195,026
1904	5,387,400	1,847,186	34.3	5,195,783
1903	4,843,228	1,486,104	30.7	5,206,973
1902	5,152,774	1,711,508	33.2	5,292,328
1901	5,276,537	1,657,237	31.4	5,389,524
Average:				
1906–1910	5,793,877	1,738,979	30.0	6,171,391
1901–1905	5,132,893	1,674,098	32.6	5,255,927

a "World" figures of production for 1906–7 to 1910–11 are based principally on official reports; the figures for 1901–2 to 1905–6 are based principally on the reports of Willet & Gray.
b Exports of sugar from the United States average less than 25,000 tons annually.

PRODUCTION AND TRADE IN AGRICULTURAL PRODUCTS.

AVERAGE ANNUAL PRODUCTION, 1906-7 TO 1910-11 (CROP YEARS).

Cane sugar.			Beet sugar.		
Country.	Long tons.	Per cent of "world" production.	Country.	Long tons.	Per cent of "world" production.
British India a	2,095,720	27.0	Germany	2,182,400	31.8
Cuba	1,450,100	18.7	Austria-Hungary d	1,357,700	19.8
Java	1,184,000	15.2	Russia (European) e	1,298,460	19.0
United States (including Hawaii and Porto Rico)	1,009,161	13.0	France f	668,360	9.8
United States	314,861	4.1	United States (continental)	425,989	6.2
Oceania b	253,940	3.3	Belgium	248,620	3.6
Brazil	246,000	3.2	Netherlands	180,600	2.6
Mauritius	207,660	2.7	Sweden	140,020	2.0
Peru	150,000	1.9	Italy	138,400	2.0
Mexico	136,580	1.7	Spain	87,000	1.3
Argentina	131,820	1.7	Denmark	70,280	1.0
Philippine Islands c	130,200	1.7	Other countries	54,860	.9
Other countries	774,600	9.9			
"World" total	7,769,781	100.0	"World" total	6,852,689	100.0

Average annual production, 1906-7 to 1910-11 (crop years)—Continued.

Average annual exports, 1906-1910 (calendar years).

All sugar.			(All sugar.)		
Country.	Long tons.	Per cent of "world" production.	Country.	Long tons.	Per cent of "world" exports.
Germany	2,182,400	14.9	Cuba	1,305,138	21.1
British India	2,095,720	14.3	Dutch East Indies	1,189,374	19.3
Cuba	1,450,100	9.9	Germany	888,845	14.4
United States (including Hawaii and Porto Rico)	1,435,150	9.8	Austria-Hungary	737,815	12.0
United States (continental)	740,850	5.1	France	254,412	4.1
Austria-Hungary	1,357,700	9.3	Mauritius	191,784	3.1
Russia (European)	1,298,460	8.9	Russia	183,007	3.0
Java	1,184,000	8.1	Belgium	153,478	2.5
France	668,360	4.6	Netherlands	147,962	2.4
Oceania	253,940	1.7	Philippine Islands	128,517	2.1
Belgium	248,620	1.7	Other countries	991,059	16.0
Brazil	246,000	1.7			
Other countries	2,202,020	15.1			
"World" total	14,622,470	100.0	"World" total	6,171,391	100.0

AVERAGE ANNUAL IMPORTS, 1906-1910 (CALENDAR YEARS).
(All sugar.)

Country.	Long tons.	Per cent of "world" imports.
United States	1,738,979	30.0
United Kingdom	1,580,602	27.3
British India	543,086	9.4
China	312,159	5.4
Canada	214,557	3.7
Japan	174,417	3.0
Turkey	135,099	2.3
France	112,509	1.9
Switzerland	90,980	1.6
Persia	88,455	1.5
Other countries	803,034	13.9
"World" total	5,793,877	100.0

a The figures represent the production of about 97 per cent of the area under sugar cane and 90 per cent of the area under all-sugar crops during 1906–7 to 1909–10.
b Includes Queensland, New South Wales, and Fiji.
c Exports for years ending June 30.
d Estimate as returned by Central Union for beet-sugar industry.
e Sugar made from beets entering factories.
f In terms of refined sugar. Average annual production of sugar and molasses in terms of refined sugar for five-year period 1906–7 to 1910–11, 678,535 long tons.

PRODUCTION AND TRADE IN AGRICULTURAL PRODUCTS. 25

TEA.

Average annual exports, 1905–1909 (calendar years).			Average annual imports, 1905–1909 (calendar years).		
Country.	Pounds.	Per cent of "world" exports.	Country.	Pounds.	Per cent of "world" imports.
British India	231,298,640	32.3	United Kingdom	272,432,607	39.5
China	198,883,467	27.7	Russia	156,130,202	22.6
Ceylon	178,567,801	24.9	United States	96,149,883	13.9
Japan (excluding Formosa)	38,945,272	5.4	Australia	30,899,511	4.5
Dutch East Indies	32,421,188	4.5	Canada	28,223,710	4.1
Formosa	23,431,775	3.3	Netherlands	9,677,157	1.4
Singapore	2,370,667	.3	Germany	8,804,534	1.3
Other countries	11,221,910	1.6	Persia	7,559,114	1.1
			New Zealand	6,516,935	.9
			British India	6,489,510	.9
			Other countries	67,294,375	9.8
"World" total	717,140,720	100.0	"World" total	690,177,538	100.0

COFFEE.

ANNUAL PRODUCTION.

Crop year.	"World."	United States (Porto Rico and Hawaii).	Per cent of "world" crop grown in United States.
	Pounds.	*Pounds.*	
1910	1,996,254,000	37,389,000	1.9
1909	2,920,212,000	47,912,000	1.6
1908	2,323,341,000	30,453,000	1.3
1907	2,744,578,000	36,698,000	1.3
1906	2,569,660,000	39,987,000	1.6
1905	2,146,253,000	30,601,000	1.4
1904	1,973,552,000	35,966,000	1.8
Average: 1905–1909	2,540,809,000	37,130,000	1.5

ANNUAL EXPORTS.

Calendar year.	"World."	United States.	Per cent of "world" exports from United States.
	Pounds.	*Pounds.*	
1910	2,163,764,874	47,159,055	2.2
1909	3,047,001,434	35,089,526	1.2
1908	2,511,684,773	34,268,012	1.4
1907	2,933,544,843	41,802,527	1.4
1906	2,687,601,738	32,821,342	1.2
1905	2,286,077,156	21,777,960	1.0
1904	2,158,661,598	25,568,821	1.2
Average: 1905–1909	2,693,181,988	33,151,873	1.2

ANNUAL IMPORTS.

Calendar year.	"World."	United States.	Per cent of "world" imports into United States.
	Pounds.	Pounds.	
1910	2,463,810,219	804,417,451	32.6
1909	2,942,428,071	1,139,826,171	38.7
1908	2,612,243,259	938,559,889	35.9
1907	2,714,932,113	940,247,312	34.6
1906	2,454,522,010	857,013,585	34.9
1905	2,348,055,342	893,889,352	38.1
1904	2,530,434,478	1,112,709,546	44.0
Average:			
1905–1909	2,614,436,159	953,907,262	36.5

AVERAGE ANNUAL PRODUCTION, 1905–1909 (CROP YEARS).

Country.	Pounds.	Per cent of "world" production.
Brazil	1,852,031,000	72.9
Venezuela	96,240,000	3.8
Guatemala	82,280,000	3.2
Colombia	79,366,000	3.1
West Indies	70,875,000	2.8
Mexico	68,688,000	2.7
Salvador	60,075,000	2.4
Dutch East Indies	59,052,000	2.3
United States [a]	37,130,000	1.5
Costa Rica	30,935,000	1.2
British India	28,680,000	1.1
Other countries	75,457,000	3.0
"World" total	2,540,809,000	100.0

AVERAGE ANNUAL EXPORTS, 1905–1909 (CALENDAR YEARS).

Country.	Pounds.	Per cent of "world" exports.
Brazil	1,852,045,203	68.8
Netherlands	171,983,466	6.4
Venezuela	96,240,252	3.6
Guatemala	75,587,534	2.8
Colombia	69,449,600	2.6
Salvador	62,620,674	2.3
Dutch East Indies	60,097,027	2.2
Haiti	55,265,080	2.1
Mexico	44,439,497	1.7
United States	33,151,873	1.2
Other countries	172,301,782	6.3
"World" total [b]	2,693,181,988	100.0

[a] Based upon exports of 35,200,000 pounds from Porto Rico and 1,930,000 pounds from Hawaii.
[b] The excess of exports and imports over production is due in a large measure to the fact that in some countries "domestic" exports include produce of foreign countries. which has become "nationalized," having been imported and become part of the domestic trade of that country.

PRODUCTION AND TRADE IN AGRICULTURAL PRODUCTS. 27

AVERAGE ANNUAL IMPORTS, 1905-1909 (CALENDAR YEARS).

Country.	Pounds.	Per cent of "world" imports.
United States	953,907,262	36.5
Germany	424,987,306	16.2
Netherlands	254,514,369	9.7
France	220,955,071	8.5
Belgium	146,066,492	5.6
Austria-Hungary	120,129,952	4.6
Sweden	74,866,518	2.9
Italy	47,400,281	1.8
United Kingdom	29,121,865	1.1
Finland	28,515,543	1.1
Other countries	313,971,500	12.0
"World" total a	2,614,436,159	100.0

a The excess of exports and imports of over production is due in a large measure to the fact that in some countries "domestic" exports include produce of foreign countries which has become "nationalized," having been imported and become part of the domestic trade of that country.

OIL CAKE AND OIL-CAKE MEAL.a

Average annual exports, 1905-1909 (calendar years).			Average annual imports, 1905-1909 (calendar years).		
Country.	Pounds.	Per cent of "world" exports.	Country.	Pounds.	Per cent of "world" imports.
United States	1,839,605,364	37.1	Germany	1,452,207,000	28.1
Russia	1,226,094,050	24.7	Denmark	943,369,114	18.3
Germany	400,296,766	8.1	United Kingdom	758,541,056	14.7
France	343,076,146	6.9	Netherlands	608,751,533	11.8
Netherlands	162,585,122	3.3	Belgium	494,023,084	9.6
Belgium	157,084,064	3.2	Sweden	276,816,551	5.4
Egypt	154,593,525	3.1	France	256,675,619	5.0
British India	147,192,931	3.0	Japan	134,407,770	2.6
China	123,863,946	2.5	Austria-Hungary	30,367,007	.6
Austria-Hungary	95,672,472	1.9	Dutch East Indies	19,056,655	.4
Other countries	308,289,063	6.2	Other countries	188,089,654	3.5
"World" total	4,958,353,449	100.0	"World" total	5,162,305,043	100.0

a Oil cake and oil-cake meal is a residue obtained in the manufacture of oil from cottonseed, flaxseed, sunflower seed, rape seed, hemp seed, peanuts, corn, soya beans, and a variety of other oleaginous seeds.

ROSIN.

Average annual exports, 1905-1909 (calendar years).			Average annual imports, 1905-1909 (calendar years).		
Country.	Pounds.	Per cent of "world" exports.	Country.	Pounds.	Per cent of "world" imports.
United States	669,830,000	80.8	Germany	238,850,608	29.3
Netherlands	71,633,305	8.6	United Kingdom	169,938,810	20.9
Germany	51,291,185	6.2	Netherlands	82,501,160	10.1
Austria-Hungary	2,894,223	.3	Austria-Hungary	72,541,912	8.9
Other countries	33,708,404	4.1	Russia	63,850,710	7.8
			Italy	31,262,110	3.8
			Brazil	28,839,683	3.5
			Argentina	23,640,476	2.9
			Canada	19,980,340	2.5
			Australia	13,407,779	1.6
			Other countries	69,988,484	8.7
"World" total	829,357,117	100.0	"World" total	814,802,072	100.0

TURPENTINE.

Average annual exports, 1905–1909 (calendar years).			Average annual imports, 1905–1909 (calendar years).		
Country.	Gallons.	Per cent of "world" exports.	Country.	Gallons.	Per cent of "world" imports.
United States	16,893,726	69.0	Germany	9,469,144	35.0
France	2,776,626	11.3	United Kingdom	7,612,456	28.1
Russia	2,049,308	8.4	Netherlands	2,930,015	10.8
Netherlands	1,534,381	6.3	Austria-Hungary	2,276,016	8.4
Germany	428,933	1.8	Canada	976,751	3.6
Other countries	808,204	3.2	Italy	880,304	3.2
			Argentina	448,269	1.7
			Australia	386,931	1.4
			Switzerland	352,997	1.3
			Russia	257,008	.9
			Other countries	1,500,709	5.6
"World" total	24,491,178	100.0	"World" total	27,090,600	100.0

INDIA RUBBER.

Average annual exports, 1905–1909 (calendar years).			Average annual imports, 1905–1909 (calendar years).		
Country.	Pounds.	Per cent of "world" exports.	Country.	Pounds.	Per cent of "world" imports.
Brazil	81,163,264	38.5	United States	74,193,026	32.2
Belgium	15,405,964	7.3	Germany	40,134,987	17.4
Germany	13,421,280	6.4	United Kingdom	30,748,861	13.4
France	13,118,018	6.2	France	22,906,951	10.0
Belgian Kongo	9,999,250	4.7	Belgium	18,897,475	8.2
Dutch East Indies	7,387,811	3.5	Russia	15,430,826	6.7
Peru	6,261,687	3.0	Netherlands	7,173,062	3.1
Singapore	5,356,507	2.5	Austria-Hungary	4,240,581	1.8
Angola	5,200,000	2.5	Italy	2,654,622	1.2
Netherlands	4,642,814	2	Canada	2,490,557	1.1
Other countries	48,811,250	2¾:2	Other countries	11,234,147	4.9
"World" total	210,767,845	100.0	"World" total	230,105,095	100.0

WOOD PULP.

Average annual exports, 1905–1909 (calendar years).			Average annual imports, 1905–1909 (calendar years).		
Country.	Pounds.	Per cent of "world" exports.	Country.	Pounds.	Per cent of "world" imports.
Norway	1,190,954,849	34.6	United Kingdom	1,486,368,128	43.3
Sweden	1,083,267,621	31.4	France	603,877,585	17.6
Canada*a*	467,600,000	13.6	United States	514,192,522	15.0
Germany	224,585,881	6.5	Belgium	234,043,042	6.8
Austria-Hungary	175,329,714	5.1	Italy	123,369,343	3.6
Finland	137,833,541	4.0	Germany	103,969,573	3.0
Belgium	62,043,694	1.8	Denmark	77,353,947	2.2
United States	23,997,425	.7	Spain	75,818,237	2.2
Switzerland	12,895,870	.4	Russia	47,122,271	1.4
Other countries	67,139,515	1.9	Argentina	36,575,849	1.1
			Other countries	130,711,171	3.8
"World" total	3,445,648,110	100.0	"World" total	3,433,401,668	100.0

a Estimated from value.

AVERAGE PRODUCTION OF AND INTERNATIONAL TRADE IN IMPORTANT AGRICULTURAL PRODUCTS.

AVERAGE ANNUAL PRODUCTION (CROP YEARS).

Product.	Five-year period.	"World."	United States.	Per cent of "world" crop grown in United States.	Relative rank of United States in "world" production.
Corn (bushels)	1905–1909	3,595,256,000	2,689,714,000	74.8	1
Wheat (bushels)	1906–1910	3,381,349,000	670,484,000	19.8	1
Wheat flour (barrels)	1906–1910				
Wheat, including wheat flour (bushels).	1906–1910				
Oats (bushels)	1906–1910	3,869,334,000	943,995,000	24.4	1
Barley (bushels)	1906–1910	1,338,663,000	169,284,000	12.6	2
Rye (bushels)	1906–1910	1,594,575,000	32,242,000	2.0	5
Potatoes (bushels)	1905–1909	5,195,008,000	307,044,000	5.9	5
Cotton (bales 478 pounds net)	1905–1909	19,728,824	11,640,551	59.0	1
Cottonseed oil (gallons)	1905–1909				
Coffee (pounds)	1905–1909	2,540,809,000	a 37,130,000	1.5	9
Flaxseed (bushels)	1905–1909	98,675,000	25,045,000	25.4	2
Rice (pounds)	1905–1909	114,095,759,000	531,989,000	0.5	10
Tobacco (pounds)	1905–1909	2,423,509,000	757,483,000	31.3	1
Hops (pounds)	1906–1910	183,527,000	47,457,000	25.9	1
Cane sugar (long tons)	1906–7, 10–11	7,769,781	314,861	4.1	4
Cane sugar (long tons)	1906–7, 10–11	7,769,781	a 1,009,161	13.0	4
Beet sugar (long tons)	1906–7, 10–11	6,852,689	425,989	6.2	5
All sugar (long tons)	1905–7, 10–11	14,622,470	740,850	5.1	8
All sugar (long tons)	1905–7, 10–11	14,622,470	a 1,435,150	9.8	4

a Including Hawaii and Porto Rico.

AVERAGE ANNUAL EXPORTS (CALENDAR YEARS).

Product.	Five-year period.	"World."	United States.	Per cent of "world" exports from United States.	Relative rank of United States in "world" exports.
Corn (bushels)	1905–1909	234,201,012	76,419,857	32.6	2
Wheat (bushels)	1906–1910	534,951,459	63,952,241	12.0	3
Wheat flour (barrels)	1906–1910	24,626,625	12,134,365	49.3	1
Wheat, including wheat flour (bushels).	1906–1910	645,771,273	118,556,884	18.4	2
Cotton (bales 478 pounds net)	1905–1909	12,695,345	8,416,503	66.3	1
Cottonseed oil (gallons)	1905–1909	55,056,550	45,445,357	82.5	1
Coffee (pounds)	1905–1909	2,693,181,988	33,151,873	1.2	10
Flaxseed (bushels)	1905–1909				
Rice (pounds)	1905–1909	11,297,164,630			
Tobacco (pounds)	1905–1909	757,727,907	320,815,134	42.3	1
Hops (pounds)	1906–1910	62,004,995	15,384,083	24.8	3
Tea (pounds)	1905–1909	717,140,720			
Oilcake and oilcake meal (pounds)	1905–1909	4,958,353,449	1,839,605,364	37.1	1
Rosin (pounds)	1905–1909	829,357,117	669,830,000	80.8	1
Turpentine (gallons)	1905–1909	24,491,178	16,893,726	69.0	1
India rubber (pounds)	1905–1909	210,767,845			
Wood pulp (pounds)	1905–1909	3,445,648,110	23,997,425	0.7	8

AVERAGE ANNUAL IMPORTS (CALENDAR YEARS).

Product	Five-year period.	"World."	United States.	Per cent of "world" imports into United States.	Relative rank of United States in "world" imports.
Corn (bushels)	1905–1909	235,885,037			
Wheat (bushels)	1906–1910	517,040,746			
Wheat flour (barrels)	1906–1910	23,183,680			
Wheat, including wheat flour (bushels)	1906–1910	621,367,306			
Cotton (bales 478 pounds net)	1905–1909	12,607,820	173,058	1.4	
Cottonseed oil (gallons)	1905–1909	55,159,280			
Coffee (pounds)	1905–1909	2,614,436,159	953,907,262	36.5	1
Flaxseed (bushels)	1905–1909				
Rice (pounds)	1905–1909	9,858,190,474	193,062,718	2.0	14
Tobacco (pounds)	1905–1909	725,973,413	38,317,922	5.3	8
Hops (pounds)	1906–1910	62,171,380	7,002,759	11.3	2
All sugar (long tons)	1906–1910	5,793,877	1,738,979	30.0	1
Tea (pounds)	1905–1909	690,177,538	96,149,883	13.9	3
Oilcake and oilcake meal (pounds)	1905–1909	5,162,305,043			
Rosin (pounds)	1905–1909	814,802,072			
Turpentine (gallons)	1905–1909	27,090,600			
India rubber (pounds)	1905–1909	230,105,095	74,193,026	32.2	1
Wood pulp (pounds)	1905–1909	3,433,401,668	514,192,522	15.0	3

RANK OF THE UNITED STATES IN THE PRODUCTION OF AND INTERNATIONAL TRADE IN SPECIFIED PRODUCTS.

Relative rank of the United States among the various countries of the world in production, exports, and imports, based upon the average statistics for a late five-year period.

Production.		Exports.		Imports.	
Corn	1	Cotton	1	Coffee	1
Wheat	1	Tobacco	1	Sugar	1
Oats	1	Wheat flour	1	India rubber	1
Cotton	1	Cottonseed oil	1	Hops	2
Tobacco	1	Oil cake and oil-cake meal	1	Tea	3
Hops	1	Rosin	1	Wood pulp	3
Barley	2	Turpentine	1	Tobacco	8
Flaxseed	2	Corn	2		
Cane sugar	4	Wheat, including wheat flour	2		
Beet sugar	5	Wheat	3		
Potatoes	5	Hops	3		
Rye	5	Wood pulp	8		
Coffee a	9	Coffee	10		
Rice	10				

a Porto Rico and Hawaii.

ADDITIONAL COPIES of this publication may be procured from the SUPERINTENDENT OF DOCUMENTS, Government Printing Office, Washington, D. C., at 5 cents per copy

CPSIA information can be obtained
at www.ICGtesting.com
Printed in the USA
LVHW031635281118
598533LV00023B/1238/P